Just A Taste That The Lord Is Good

Chapbook Press

Schuler Books
2660 28th Street SE
Grand Rapids, MI 49512
(616) 942-7330
www.schulerbooks.com

Just a Taste that the Lord is Good

ISBN 13: 9781948237727

Library of Congress Control Number: in file

© 2021, Robert Parson

All rights reserved. No part of this book may be reproduced, stored in a retrieval system, or transmitted in any form or by any means, electronic, mechanical, photocopying, recording or otherwise, except for the purpose of brief reviews, without the prior written permission of the author.

Printed in the United States by Chapbook Press.

Preface

I lead a life of rebellion against God until I was thirty-seven; why God has allowed me to try to honor Him with words of praise and worship in this book of poems I still don't understand.

It just proves even more God's goodness His mercy and His grace. I feel so unworthy and yet so privileged. I pray He will be glorified and whoever reads this book will understand more about His greatness. I know nothing I have written can even come close to describing His magnificence.

In appreciation for His great love and salvation, I dedicate this book to my Heavenly Father and give Him all the praise and glory. May His Son Jesus be lifted up and draw all who will believe to himself. May we all praise Him more for He is worthy of all our praise and all our honor, and I thank Him for paying the price for my soul.

With my deepest love and gratitude, thank you Lord.

Table Of Contents

THE RED WHITE AND BLUE	7
AN OLD MAN'S PRAYER	8
LORD I THANK YOU	10
A BEAUTIFUL DAY	11
A CRY WENT OUT	12
A PLACE WHERE EVERYONE GOES	13
A LOG HOME BESIDE THE CRYSTAL SEA	14
WHATEVER THE LORD PLEASED	16
BEND THE KNEE	17
I AM AMAZED	18
HELP ME TO BE PATIENT	19
DON'T LET ANOTHER CHILD DIE	20
HIS SPIRIT IS OUR GUIDE	22
HOLINESS OR FOOLISHNESS	24
HOW WILL THEY KNOW	25
JOIN US AND SEE	26
MY VEXED SOUL	27
PRAYER FOR MY BROTHER	28
THE ARMOR OF GOD	30
THE ESSENCE OF YOUR PRESENCE	31
THE LORD IS COMING	32
THERE'S A BATTLE RAGING	34
FOLLOWERS	35
TO HIS GLORY	36
WASTED FRUIT	37
WHERE WOULD I BE WITHOUT THE LOVE OF GOD	38
A SURE FOUNDATION	39
WHAT A FOOL I'VE BEEN	40
EVERY DAY IS CHRISTMAS	42
GOING BEYOND	43
CLUTTERED HEARTS	44
I AM SAD	46

I HUMBLY PRAISE YOU	47
IN A LITTLE ROOM	48
STANDING WITH OUR LORD	50
THE ENEMY DEFEATED	51
THE HEART OF GOD	52
THE ROOTS OF OUR NATION	53
WHERE WILL WE FIND GOD'S LOVE?	54

THE RED WHITE AND BLUE

We thank You, Lord, for the Red, White, and Blue.
But without Your love, what would we do?
We're the home of the brave, and the land of the free,
But it's through Your Son Jesus that we have true liberty.
Help us, Father, to be united to stand
In unity as we obey Your command
To love one another and put You first,
And for Your righteousness to hunger and thirst.
On our money we put, "In God we trust."
Please help us, Lord, not to covet and lust,
After the things of the world, that take us from You,
Not understanding the meaning of the Red, White, and Blue.
The Red's for the courage it took to go to the cross.
The White's for the purity there that was lost
When You took our sins so we could be free
And live with You throughout eternity.
The Blue is for perseverance and justice, they say.
You showed us Your love and commitment that day,
When You gave Your life at dark Calvary,
So we could understand true love and equity.
So we thank You, Lord, for the Red, White and Blue,
And as we look to it, may it remind us of You:
One nation under God, liberty and justice for all.
And may we always be free Jesus, on Your name to call.

AN OLD MAN'S PRAYER

On a dark and dreary day
An old man knelt down to pray,
And in heaviness of heart
He didn't know where to start.
Finally in desperation
He said, "O, God of all creation,
if you can hear my cry,
Please don't let me die.
I know my life has been
Wasted with much sin,
And now that I am old,
My heart is calloused and cold.
But I remember when I was young,
A man told me about Your Son.
He said that He had died for me,
I think He said at Calvary.
I remember He said He rose again,
And something about payment for sin.
And if I would believe in Him,
Then I could be born again.
I think I believe that this is true,
He said He was a reflection of You.
And I know You created the beauty I see,
So maybe You could recreate me.
I'm sorry for the things I've done,
And I thank you for sending Your Son,
And I'm sorry to come to You in tears,

But I realize I've wasted all these years.
And I hope I'm not too old,
Or have committed too much sin
To ask that You forgive me,
And let me be born again.
Well, I hope You heard my pleas,
And I hope I can get off my knees.
But I want to come back again,
And I hope You'll let me in.
I can't tell You what a pleasure it's been
To come to You this way.
I wasn't sure I could talk to You,
And I didn't know what to say.
But now that I kind of know You,
I hope to come to You each day.
And maybe by the next time,
I'll know better how to pray."

LORD, I THANK YOU

Lord, I thank You that I heard Your Word, thank You for the Word I heard.
When I heard a voice sing praises to Your name,
Then I understood Your love for me. I understood You cared for me,
And I realized the purpose for my life, is to glorify Your Son with praise,
Lifting up His holy name always.
Giving thanks to You for what Your Son has done.
He has given everything to me, laying down His life for me
When He bore my shame and went to Calvary's tree.
Help me understand His pain, so I can glorify His name,
For His name is great and greatly to be praised.
Give me boldness to proclaim His name. In His love not be ashamed
Because His love is great and greatly to be praised.

A BEAUTIFUL DAY

Good morning, Lord, what a beautiful day.
I'm glad I decided to take time to pray.
To come to You and thank You again,
For all of Your love, and forgiveness of sin.
And I can't think of a better way, to start a beautiful day,
Than to kneel down before You and pray,
And to come to You with gladness of heart,
With joy and with singing, the new day to start.
The birds, are all singing their chorus of song.
Their joyful chirping, they sing all day long.
The fish are jumping. I guess they're glad too.
The cows join in with an occasional moo.
The chickens are crowing and clucking away.
They're thanking You too for a beautiful day.
Off in the distance I hear a coyote howl,
The bark of a dog, and the hoot of an owl.
Oh, what a glorious day this will be,
And to think it all started from my bed to my knee.
Me talking to You, and You talking to me.
Yes, what a beautiful day this will be.

A CRY WENT OUT

Help me, Lord, a cry went out.
Help me, Lord, I began to shout.
Help me, Lord, to obey
Your precious Word every day.
Help me, Lord, to understand.
Please hear the cries of this man.
Wisdom and knowledge is my desire.
Faith and love is what You require.
How can I be in fellowship with You,
When it's the evil of my heart that I do.
Help me, Lord, I cried again.
Please cleanse my heart of all its sin.
And help me to make right choices,
And not listen to other voices
That lead me away from You.
Without You, Lord, what would I do?

these years.
o old,
nuch sin
'e me,
gain.
ny pleas,
ny knees.
 again,
me in.
ure it's been
way.
 to You,
t to say.
ow You,
ach day.
t time,
 pray."

A PLACE WHERE EVERYONE GOES

I once went to a place,
A place where everyone goes.
Now it's a place called Happiness,
A place that everyone knows.
Make every place a happy place,
By having Jesus in your souls.
I once went to a place,
A place where everyone goes.
Now it's a place called Loneliness,
A place that everyone knows.
But I made that a happy place,
By having Jesus in my soul.
Now listen to me, friend,
And try to understand,
This world could be a paradise,
For all women and all men.
But listen to this, too,
Because there's something you have to know.
This world can be a hell, without Jesus in your soul.
It can be a pure old hell, without Him in your soul,
And you're going to go to hell, without Him in your soul.
If you don't want to go to hell, you'd better get Him in your soul.

A LOG HOME BESIDE THE CRYSTAL SEA

Help me, Lord, overcome the pain,
In my heart, from all the rain.
Dark clouds shadow from above.
I need some of Your precious love.
Tempests blowing everywhere,
Puts in my heart a dreadful scare,
And only You can calm the fear,
When I feel Your presence near.
Your precious love so dear.
A peace that passes understanding.
A love so sweet and undemanding,
And when the storm is passed,
Your love I found at last.
The tempest finally done,
The love is Your own Son.
Precious in your sight,
Lights up the darkest night.
No more shadow over me,
No more tempest from the sea,
The brightness of His love I share,
With scared and lonely people everywhere.
A gentle breeze of light and love,
You brought us from Your home above,
Where someday You will walk with me,
Beside the waters of the crystal sea.
Along the shores of the crystal sea,
A glorious day that will be,
When my Jesus I shall see.

For now we walk by faith alone,
And Your promise of that heavenly home.
Oh, what a day that will be,
When that heavenly home I see,
The one that You prepared for me,
A glorious place that will erase,
All the pain and sorrow and tears,
That I have felt throughout the years.
All of this I will remember no more,
When I reach that heavenly shore.
That place You prepared for me,
A log home beside the crystal sea.

WHATEVER THE LORD PLEASED

Whatever the Lord pleased,
That He did in Heaven,
And in the earth, and in the seas.
He made the moon and the stars,
The birds and the bees,
The mountains and all the trees.
He made a stinky little skunk,
An elephant with a trunk.
A deer and a goat and fleas,
A bat and a rat and a long-tailed cat.
A horse and some chimpanzees.
He made a dog and a frog and a pig and hog
And a snake without no knees.
He made a moose and a goose, a bear and a hare
And then He made you for me.
And then He made you for me.

BEND THE KNEE

I believe my Lord died for me,
So I can live with Him throughout eternity.
My sins He took to Calvary,
To be nailed to that cursed tree,
So I could have the victory,
Over death and hell and stupidity.
But it's not just a life of leisure and ease,
But of sacrifice, down on my knees.
Or to live for self, my flesh to please,
But to live for Him and meet others needs.
But I'm so blind I can't see
The way to get the victory.
Give me light. This is my plea.
The answer came, "bend the knee."
How can I come before You any other way,
Than on my knees, to make my pleas.
That's how I have to pray,
And not just when I feel like it,
But every single day.
No wonder I was blind,
No strength could I find,
No power for my life,
No weapon for my fight.
My sin I couldn't see,
A sin I forgot to confess,
It's the sin of prayerlessness.

I AM AMAZED

I am amazed the way You touch my heart and take my pain.
I am amazed the way You bring the sunshine after a rain.
I am amazed the joy that floods my soul when You are near.
I am amazed the love I could not see, I now see clear.
I am amazed the peace that rules my life that You have brought.
I am amazed the things I could not learn, I've now been taught.
I am amazed the spirit of Your love you gave to me.
I am amazed the way that Your word has made me free.
I am amazed of all the souls on earth, why save me?
I am amazed You gave Your life for me at Calvary.
And I am amazed that I am amazed.

HELP ME TO BE PATIENT

Lord, help me to be patient
And always wait on You.
And help me to understand,
What You are trying to do.
Help me yield my life a sacrifice,
Holy, always loving You.
And keep my mind on things above,
And to reach out to others with Your love.
Your Word to do and share
With people everywhere.
And keep Your light within my heart,
So my pathway does not get dark.
Help me always to be in prayer,
And feel Your Presence always there.
Without You, I can do nothing at all,
When I walk in the dark, I fall.
And without Your Presence near,
Your voice I couldn't hear,
If Your Word I didn't know,
I wouldn't know the way to go.
And Your love I couldn't show
To others who don't know.
So help me to be patient
And always wait on You,
So when others see my life,
They'll see that You're there too.

DON'T LET ANOTHER CHILD DIE

There's a dreadful cry throughout the earth.
It seems human life has very little worth.
It's taken like a grain of salt.
It's taken and no one's at fault.
How can this be, why can't we see
The love and joy a child can bring,
Their beautiful smiles, the songs they sing,
That lifts our spirits when passed along.
To take that from us, it has to be wrong.
We know our life is precious and dear,
But to that cry, we give a deaf ear.
If it were us, would we be so blind?
If it were our life on the line,
Would we want others to just pass by?
Wouldn't we want them to hear our cry?
How can this be, why can't we see?
Isn't life dear to you and me?
If we don't care, how can we share
Our love with those we do not hear?
Or do we even love at all?
Or is life just a game we play,
Life golf or soccer or basketball?
It seems like that's what we think,
As deeper and deeper in sin we sink.
As farther and farther from God we go,
Our lives are like a TV show.
We watch it for a little while,
We laugh and grin and smile,
And then when it comes to an end,
We regret where we've been.

Doesn't every child deserve a chance
To laugh and run and sing and dance?
What if you weren't here
To touch the lives that you hold dear?
Who could ever take your place,
The memories they can't erase?
Listen and you will hear the cry,
And don't let another child die.
It's up to us to stop it now.
Listen to God and He will show us how.

HIS SPIRIT IS OUR GUIDE

The Spirit is my guide,
When in the Lord I abide.
He teaches me His Word,
And brings to remembrance,
The things I heard.
He comforts me when I worry,
And tells me not to hurry.
Wait on the Lord, meditate on His Word.
And yield yourself to the things you read and heard.
The joy of the Lord will be your strength,
When you come to His fountain and drink.
A spring of water, fresh and pure,
Giving us strength to endure,
The things of life we incur.
When all our hope seems gone,
He brings to mind a song,
"Jesus loves me, this I know,
for the Bible tells Me so."
Without His Spirit where would I be?
Like a ship lost at sea,
With waves of doubt overcoming me,
The love of God unable to see.
It's the Spirit that draws me to His side,
And hides me in the crimson tide,
Where nothing harmful can abide,
Where I'm sealed with love for evermore.
An island with a heavenly shore,
And Jesus is the only door.
Nothing evil can come in.
No fear, or doubt, or any sin.

Only joy and peace and love.
The Spirit of God, a pure white dove.

HOLINESS OR FOOLISHNESS

Oh, Lord, my God, help me see
What my sin has done to me.
And even more, what it has done to Thee.
And to Your Son, who was so pure,
Until my sin He chose to endure.
And take it on Himself, giving up all of His wealth,
And for me, He became poor,
When my sin and shame He bore.
So He could sanctify me,
And through His blood, I could become holy.
And help me to see what He went through,
So I can better obey You, and do the things You told me to.
Or for my life, it will be a loss, that Jesus died and went to the cross.
If I continue to live in sin, not caring that they crucified Him.
If I don't surrender my life to You,
And do the things You want me to,
Then I don't really believe in Him,
That He died to take away my sin.
A disregard for what He went through,
Won't make me holy, but instead, a fool.

HOW WILL THEY KNOW

How will they know if we don't go.
How will they see if we don't plea,
The cause of Christ across the sea.
How will they understand,
If there's no willingness of man
To show the love of God that is free.
Will you go, will you help them see?
Don't you understand, those men are you and me.
But first we must start
With a willingness of heart,
To give up the things we cherish,
The things that soon shall perish.
Then we're able to see
The things that count for eternity.
Then this could be our plea,
Here I am, Lord, send me.

JOIN US AND SEE

The darkness has come, you cannot see.
Come to the light, this is God's plea.
Take truth by the hand, then you will see
The love of my God, then you'll be free.
To walk in the light with love and with peace,
Your joy will be full, your love will increase.
You'll reach out for others, to bring them along.
They'll see by your love you mean them no wrong.
They'll feel by your touch, your gentle embrace,
They'll know by your smile, and the warmth of your face.
Then tears will be mingled, their fears they will share,
When they see that you love them,
And you really do care.
They'll see the light too,
Then darkness will fade.
And they will reach out to others,
With the new friend they made.
The light will get brighter as more come along.
Our joy will increase, our love will get strong.
We'll lift up our voices a chorus of song,
To reach out yet farther as more come along.
How far will it go? It's all up to you.
Don't walk in the darkness, we love you too.
Join us and see, our love will increase.
How far will it go, till all are at peace?

MY VEXED SOUL

Years I spent vexing my soul, letting any old thought take control.
Not caring that you died for me so I could have the victory,
And that I could walk in peace and I could be free.
I don't really know what I believed. It was like something had control of me.
And I was held in captivity; years I spent in vanity,
Not caring about Your love for me.
And then one day at my lowest despair,
I said a little prayer called Your name and You were there
As I humbled myself and cried out to You,
Your everlasting love came shining through
The weight of sin was lifted that day when I believed in You Jesus,
And started to pray
Now my thoughts You control. My mind is clear and so is my soul
There is praise on my lips and joy in my heart,
Singing and praising each new day I start.
Thank you, God for not letting me go and for Jesus the love of my soul.

PRAYER FOR MY BROTHER

In a little room, far away,
A person was crying one day,
And on his knees he made his pleas,
For one that had gone astray.
Oh, Lord, my God, I come to You,
With humbleness of heart.
My brother is lost and dying,
Because he chose from You to depart.
I know, dear Lord, I'm not worthy,
To come to you this way,
Because in my heart, I chose to depart,
And go my own selfish way.
But when I came to my senses,
Repented and found forgiveness,
You told me that I could pray,
So now that I'm before You,
Uncertain of what I should say,
I ask that you forgive me, and teach me how to pray.
I come to You in tears,
Because I wasted a lot of years.
Why waste another day?
For I wish I were accursed from Christ,
For my brother to find his way.
I know, dear Lord, You died for all,
But why me have you chose to save?
I've wasted all my living
On a life that was depraved.

Help me now from this day forth,
From sin not to be enslaved.
And deliver me from my foolish thoughts,
And the lustful things I've craved.
And teach me, Lord, not to be ashamed
Of the Gospel of which I'm saved.
For it's the power of God unto salvation,
To all who will believe,
And the way to come before You,
And the sinful life to leave.
How blessed is Your Word,
And the joy that it can bring.
It's brought my heart for crying,
And taught me how to sing.
I praise You, Lord, for what You have done.
I praise You, Lord, for Christ Your Son.
I know, dear Lord, my brother You'll save,
when I surrender my life, and become Your slave.

THE ARMOR OF GOD

When our minds are set on things above,
And we're seeking His kingdom first,
His Word will be a delight to us,
And for righteousness we will thirst.
He will add to us the things we need,
Like water and food and clothes,
When we have the mind of Christ,
And His love through us shows.
His Spirit will guide us and give us light,
When we use His Word, a Sword to fight.
When we're clothed in His armor, we will not fail,
And the gates of hell will not prevail.
So stand therefore, your loins girded with Truth,
And the Breastplate of Righteousness in front of you.
You feet shod with the Gospel of Peace
And with the Shield of Faith, our love will increase.
We will see the fiery darts of the wicked quenched before our face
And we will take up the Helmet of Salvation, and put it in its place.
We will take the Sword of the Spirit, which is the Word of God,
And when praying in the Spirit over evil we will trod.
We will see the lost get clothed in white,
When they get saved and join the fight.
At the end of it all we will be with God's Son,
And we will hear the words, "Sit down; well done."

THE ESSENCE OF YOUR PRESENCE

The essence of Your presence
Floods my heart with love
And overflowing joy
That helps me rise above
All my cares and troubles,
All my worries and woes,
All of the things that concern me,
That no one else knows.
Only You can do this, only when You are near.
The voice of the Holy Spirit
Is the only thing I hear.
Until I hear Your voice,
The anticipation's there.
Will the words "Well done!"
Be the words I hear?
Every time I think so, I fight back another tear.
How can I be so blessed to know someone like You?
Someone who is so loving in everything you do?
You gave your life on Calvary to save someone like me,
Hanging there, bleeding and dying, on that cursed tree.
When all my life I've cursed You, and took Your name in vain,
Not thinking that You went there to take away my pain.
Not caring that You died to pay for all my sin
For an entrance into Heaven, that I may enter in.
Now I praise Your Name to everyone that's here,
And tell them of my Savior, the One that is so near.
And I pray they understand the essence of your presence.
You're holding me in Your hand.

THE LORD IS COMING

I know the Lord is coming
Yes, He's coming back again.
I know my Lord is coming,
But I really don't know when.
He's coming to take me to a place I've never been.
I know the Lord is coming.
Yes, He's coming back again.
Do you know Him as your Saviour?
Do you know Him as your Friend?
Are you trusting in His blood
To cleanse you from your sin?
If you want to go to Heaven,
Then you must be born again.
I know my Lord is coming,
But I really can't say when.
Now He told me things I would see
At the coming of the end:
The wars, the plagues, the famines,
The earthquakes and the sin.
He said that some would leave Him,
And go back to where they had been.
Like a dog returns to vomit,
They go back into their sin.
Now you better think things over,
And don't let your love grow colder.
Can't you see the time's at hand
For the end of wicked man?

You better stop and see
Where you'll spend eternity.
If you know the Lord is coming,
You better listen to my plea.
Because I know my Lord is coming
Yes, He's coming back for me.
I know my Lord is coming,
Because He's coming back for me.

THERE'S A BATTLE RAGING

There's a battle raging inside my soul,
And it's left me wounded with a gaping hole.
The pain is great and hard to endure,
And I'm praying to God to send me a cure.
There will be more wounds of this, I'm sure.
It started back a long time ago,
When I set my heart on His Word to know.
I'm fighting an enemy I can't see,
So it's easy for him to get the best of me.
I have the weapons God gave to me,
But because of the darkness of my heart, I can't see.
My will is strong, I want to win,
But the enemy advances each time I sin.
Finally I'm starting to understand,
There's more than one enemy fighting each man.
His Word brought me light, and now I can see,
The lust of my flesh is my worst enemy.
Thank you, Lord, for sending your cure.
Please help me now to covet no more.
And please close the wound that is still open and sore,
And pour in the oil, so I sin there no more.

FOLLOWERS

Going to church doesn't make me a Christian, a follower of Christ I must be.
Yielding myself to the things that he taught in lowliness and humility,
Always praying and thanking my Lord for the things I now start to see,
The faults of my heart, the filth of my mind, and the works of the enemy.
The fear of the Lord is the beginning of knowledge,
But fools despise wisdom and instruction.
The thoughts of the flesh are sorrow and pain and always lead to destruction.
The fear of the Lord is the beginning of wisdom, and the knowledge of the holy to understand.
The unbelieving heart goes away from that truth and lives like destructive man.
You would think we would learn from the mistakes we have made,
But the enemy has blinded our hearts.
To keep us from the abundant life and from the love of the Lord to depart.
The moral of the story is plain to see to those who will believe:
Trust in the Lord with all your heart and don't give a place for the enemy.

TO HIS GLORY

God was, and is, and always will be.
He spoke and created all that we see.
The earth beneath, the heavens above,
All that He did, He did out of love.
He created a man, then gave him a wife,
To be his friend and helpmate for life,
To have his children, and replenish the earth,
To work by his side, and show him her worth.
He gave us His Word, and planted His seed,
The Holy Scriptures, all that we need
To examine our hearts and show us our sin,
So we could repent and be born again.
He gave us His Spirit to guide us along,
And convict our hearts when we do wrong.
His Son He sent to pay for our sin,
So we could have fellowship with Him again.
Oh, what love our Father has given,
Sending His Son from His home in heaven,
To pay for our sins at dark Calvary,
To be spit on and mocked, and nailed to a tree.
Eternity in hell my payment would be,
If Jesus wouldn't have paid it for me.
I don't understand, I'm only a man,
Made from the dust, and filled with my lust.
Why would He let Jesus die for me?
So I could tell you this story, and give Him the glory.

WASTED FRUIT

So much fruit is going to waste,
Because the words of God are bitter to our taste.
And the things of earth seem pleasant and sweet,
Till we peel back the covering, and reveal the defeat.
No strength for my spirit in earth will I find,
No food for my soul, no peace for my mind,
Just bitter regret at another lost day.
No fruit for my spirit, no joy for my pay,
My carnal thoughts have done it again,
I fed them all day, and let them win.
The Spirit kept saying "Let me have control,
Or at the end of the day, there'll be a hole in your soul."
An emptiness with only one end,
The taste of regret, and the shame of my sin.
Why don't I listen to the things that are right,
And obey God's Word and not put up a fight?
At the end of my life, I'll look back and see
All of the fruit my Lord had there for me.

WHERE WOULD I BE WITHOUT THE LOVE OF GOD

I will worship Him wherever I may go.
I will worship Him with all my heart and soul.
Where would I be without the love of God?
Where would my path lead, what road would I be on?
How would I know true love? How would I know His Son?
Where would I find peace? Where would my joy come from?
Who would I turn to, when everything goes wrong?
What would I sing about, if I didn't sing His songs?
And how could I worship Him, if I didn't know His Son?
So I will worship Him with everything I am.
I will worship Him as long as I can stand.
I will worship Him, I will get down on my knees.
I'll worship Him because it's God I want to please.

A SURE FOUNDATION

A sure foundation I have found. It is given by the Lord.
I am now standing on Holy ground, God's unchanging everlasting Word.
Upon this rock I make my base, a fortress for my soul,
The storms of life cannot displace though mighty billows roll.
A hiding place for many a man from life's relentless blast,
It has stood the test of time and throughout time it will last.
It is free to all who will believe in Him and will trust Him from their heart,
Salvation for your soul, God's Word with joy He will impart.
A Guide and a Friend through the test of life, now He has become,
True and just I thank Him now He brought me through every one.
Over and over I have come to Him, He never has denied.
With gentle words, gentle hands, and arms that are open wide,
He touched my life so deeply; He anchored me in His love.
By chords of love, He secured me till I reached my home above,
A home that he has prepared for me, a mansion by the crystal sea,
A glorious place where I will be with him throughout eternity.

WHAT A FOOL I'VE BEEN

Oh, what a fool I've been, to walk again in sin,
When once I walked in peace and love
In fellowship with my Lord above.
How could I leave the comfort He gave?
A dreadful soul He chose to save.
Nowhere could I find a love so kind,
So sweet and true.
Without You, Lord, what would I do?
Face my ugly sin alone,
Forget the love that You have shown.
The pain and shame that you endured
To save a lost and dying world.
Why can't we see the love You've given?
Your Son, who left His home in Heaven,
Our sin and shame to bear, that we commit everywhere.
Without thinking what we have done,
Our sins crucified Your only Son.
How can we be so blind with pride?
It's for our transgressions that He died,
And suffered on that cursed tree.
It's our sins He bore, yes, you and me.
We're the ones who put Him there,
All because we don't care
That our hearts are full of sin,
That we commit again and again.
Lost without hope is where we would be,
If Jesus hadn't gone to Calvary
To be nailed to that cursed tree
For the sins of you and me.
Oh, what love that He has shown,

Hanging there, dying all alone
To cleanse our hearts within,
And save us from the payment of sin.
Hell to all who don't believe,
A gift from God they don't receive.
What more could He have done?
He gave the world His only Son.
Listen to me now, my friend,
And remember what a fool I've been,
And don't you dare return to your sin.

EVERY DAY IS CHRISTMAS

Every day is Christmas if Jesus is your Friend.
A new gift every morning and life without end.
A love that endures forever, a peace we can't understand.
And the joy that we share as we walk hand-in-hand.
Excitement as we wonder what joy this new day will bring,
As we talk with Him in prayer and worship Him as we sing.
Glory to God in the highest, peace and good will toward men,
Every day is Christmas if Jesus is your Friend.
So bow your head before Him, thank Him every day
For the gift of life he gave you and the joy he brought your way.
Open your eyes and receive it;
His love is never far and even if you don't feel it,
No matter where you are Jesus gave you life and He gave His life for you.
He is always there to forgive you no matter what you do,
So humble yourself before Him, bow your head and pray.
Jesus is your friend and Christmas is today.
Every day is Christmas if Jesus is your Friend.
A new gift every morning and life without end.

GOING BEYOND

It is time to go beyond what we see and feel and think.
It is time to come to your fountain of water and drink
Waters of life like an ocean I see.
I am like a grain of sand as it washes over me.
Waves of Your love cleanse my soul as it purifies and
makes me whole.
I want to fear. I feel so small.
Your love is so great, so wide and so tall.
It reaches beyond the boundaries of time,
It flows through my heart and cleanses my mind.
I can't see its end,
I can't feel its depth, I can't imagine its worth.
It's worth more than life's breath.
If words could express what Your love has done for me,
It would take from now though eternity
To tell everyone what it means to me.
To know You, Jesus, is to really see
The heart of God and the heart of man
And why You died for me I now understand.
Your love is for all you want me to proclaim,
Your love is pure and always the same.
Your love and Your Word are bound by Your name.
Nothing is greater and now I see,
A reflection of You is what You want me to be.
Letting Your love shine through me so others will
Proclaim it throughout eternity.

CLUTTERED HEARTS

Our hearts are cluttered and blackened with sin.
We need to repent and be born again.
We are so full of self, the light can't get in.
We think we know so we don't humble ourselves.
We work for pennies and overlook true wealth.
We have no love or joy or peace,
But bitterness and anger and hate have increased.
We see the evil and the filth on the earth
But not the treasures that can bring us true worth.
Wisdom and knowledge and understanding have ceased,
But sex and violence and covetousness have increased.
Our gods are our televisions and our computers, it seems.
Our jobs and our hobbies and our sports are our dreams.
Our actions are the energy of our thoughts, you see.
It's getting worse and worse. Because of you and me,
Our minds have been tricked by our enemy and foe.
He only gives us what he wants us to know.
How can this be? Why can't we see
The evil that is overcoming you and me?
The truth is near, but we don't want to hear
that our minds and our thoughts have been deceived.
That things are getting worse because of what we believed.
When love is the motive for what we do,
The light will get brighter and start to shine through.
We will see the truth and start to understand:
We need to trust in God's Word and not in man.
Man tells us he will make things easier, so we have more time.
Yet, we are all so busy we are destroying our mind.

We don't stop to think that is what we have done.
But it is all for self, not to honor God's Son.
How far will it go and who will win your soul?
Or do you think that you really want to know?

I AM SAD

I am sad today because they say another child has been taken away.
She was taken when she went out to play by an evil man they say.
On a bright and beautiful sunny day her life was taken away,
Her beautiful smile now gone but her memory will live on and on
In the hearts of those who care who lifted her up to God in prayer.
And now we try to understand the evil that is throughout our land,
That's in the hearts of evil men, the evil that we have let in
When we turned from God and back to sin that we commit again and again.
Our hearts are so dark we can't understand.
How did this evil get into our land?
We left God's commandments and trusted in man,
Who has taken them out of our schools, and now we have become fools.
Now we are reaping what we have sown, an evil like we have never known,
Our children even taken right out of our homes.
It is getting worse and worse as on we go, pornography on every show,
Teaching the mind of evil man sex and violence are ok.
Watch what you want as long as you pay, now we all pay for what they do.
Turn back to God; don't be a fool; get the commandments back in the school.
Teach the children the golden rule,
Do unto others as you have them do to you.
It is time for Christians to take a stand,
Turn from the evil that is in our land,
And pray to God that the world would understand .
Our mind is a sacred place for God to command 2 Chronicles-7:14

I HUMBLY PRAISE YOU

I humbly bow before You Lord and I lift my voice in praise,
For the love that You have brought me and the joy of all my days.
To thank You for Your blessings and the peace that we now share.
My thoughts are on Your presence and You always meet me there.
The sweetness of Your voice is all that I can hear.
My heart starts beating faster and I know that You are near.
To touch my mind and assure me that I am now made whole.
Forever in Your presence Your love has cleansed my soul.
Now every day I thank You with the words that I now sing,
Remembering every moment the joy that You now bring.
When You touched my thoughts and healed me, now Your love I know,
Your spirit lives within me, Your peace now takes control.
Forever in Your presence Your love has cleansed my soul.
Now I thank You every morning my heart I want to show.
Forever in Your presence Your love has cleansed my soul.

IN A LITTLE ROOM

In a little room far away a little girl knelt down to pray,
For her daddy who had gone to war,
Knowing she would not see him anymore.
As tears trickled down her little cheek
And melted in her mouth, she started to speak.
She folded her hands and lifted her eyes,
Remembering when they had said their goodbyes.
He said that he loved her and it would be all right,
And that her Heavenly Father would keep her safe at night.
That her mom would tuck her in while he was away,
And Jesus would keep her safe day by day.
She knew her daddy would not lie and that he would not
want her to cry.
But she could not help the feelings inside,
When they got the news that her daddy had died.
Jesus, I know my daddy is with You tonight,
And I was wondering if it would be all right
If You would tell him I love him and that I am being good,
Just like I promised I would.
If You would send an angel to be with my mom,
To comfort her and keep her calm.
She cries a lot and it makes me sad,
She doesn't understand You are taking care of my dad.
I know she misses him and so do I, but it hurts real bad to
see her cry.
In a little room not far away a widow and mother knelt
down to pray.
As she folded her hands and started to speak,
Tears ran down the side of her cheek,
And melted in her mouth as she started to speak.

Jesus, I know my husband is with you tonight,
And I know everything is going to be all right.
Your Word like an angel has flooded my soul,
Your peace and your grace have made me whole.
I was wondering if it would be all right
if you could tuck my daughter in tonight
and let her know everything is all right.

STANDING WITH OUR LORD

To stand with our Lord takes courage and truth,
Being pure in heart His love is our guide.
The proof of His love is His hands, feet and His side.
Our test will be not to move from that truth
And to extend His love will be our proof.
Our thoughts and our words the thief wants to steal.
To take them away how will they know love is real.
Our action the energy of our thoughts they will see,
When we lay down our life and love our enemy.
The wounds have been many but the spirit lives on,
Through the lives of believers who cherish the Son.
His blood and His Word we carry through time,
Cleansing man's soul's and renewing their minds.
The labor is hard and the pay seems small,
But the reward at the end will be worth it all.
The Lord Himself will set us down,
A robe a ring a mansion and crown.
Will be given to those who shared His love,
And everlasting life with our Father above.

THE ENEMY DEFEATED

You're in a trap, you're in a snare, you're in the devil's lair.
He has your thoughts, you can't escape. Your mind is always there.
Your actions too, he is working through
To do his deadly deeds. to keep your mind on his thoughts,
That is how he succeeds.
You can't escape, that's what you think, but friend you just don't know,
The devil has been defeated by a King who is His foe.
And His blood He gave on Calvary, to wash you white as snow
And His Word is truth, you are made clean, so don't think that way again.
Confessing now what you have done, Jesus forgives you all your sin.
Start thanking God, He is the One, who teaches you the way to go
And keep your thoughts on His Word, your mind is now made whole.

THE HEART OF GOD

The heart of God is His Word and His Son.
The Spirit is love and all Three are One.
The beat of His heart is peace towards men.
Good will and truth throughout the land,
O, that we hear it what joy would it bring.
To sing hallelujah to our Lord and King,
With blessings and mercy and grace at His hand.
He reaches from heaven to give to each man.
To receive and to know it is just to believe.
The gift is extended our hearts must receive,
The heart of our Father will then beat in us.
To reach out to others who never had heard,
The love of our Father is His Son and His Word.

THE ROOTS OF OUR NATION

The roots of a tree is its life and its strength,
The taller the tree the deeper the roots sink.
Take away the roots the tree cannot stand.
Cut the roots death will be slow.
The fruit will not come the sap will not flow.
No leaves for its beauty no buds for new life.
No shade for the weary away from the strife.
The roots of our love is its life and its strength.
The more we love the deeper they sink.
Take away the roots our love cannot stand.
Cut the roots the death will be slow.
The fruit will not come the love will not grow.
No leaves for its beauty no buds for new life.
No shade for the weary away from the strife.
The God of our nation is its life and its strength.
The more trust in God the less we will sink.
Take away our God our nation cannot stand.
Cut our roots the death will be slow.
The love will not come but the evil will flow.
No honor for His beauty no spirit for new life.
No harbor for the weary away from the strife.

WHERE WILL WE FIND GOD'S LOVE?

The Lord has blessed me in so many ways.
He put joy in my heart where Jesus stays.
He surrounded me with people who care,
And showed me how my love to share.
I thank Him for His spirit within,
That convinces my heart of hidden sin.
I thank Him for His Word each day,
That shows me how to walk in His way.
And teaches me what I should say,
When I talk with others and when I pray.
I'm thankful that He hears my cry,
And I'll be with Him when I die.
I thank Him for the blessings given,
And the assurance of my home in heaven.
If words could express all that He's given,
The world couldn't hold the things written.
Never has someone so dear,
Brought so much hope and love and cheer.
To a darkened world stained with sin,
Where deceits lie without and within.
Where Satan lies in wait to deceive,
And destroy the lives of those who don't believe.
Where sex and crime and violence and death,
Are the thoughts of men and on their breath.
They watch it everyday on TV's,
Till it infects the heart like a disease.

They act it out on our city streets,
With the unsuspected people they meet,
Who's in control does anyone know?
Our lives are like a television show.
Who writes the things our children see?
Is it people like you and me?
No wonder things are the way they are,
To see the evil we don't have to look far.
A reflection of the things within,
That's why this world is full of sin.
Our hearts we let Satan deceive,
All because we don't receive
The Son of God who loves us so.
We won't find that love on a television show.

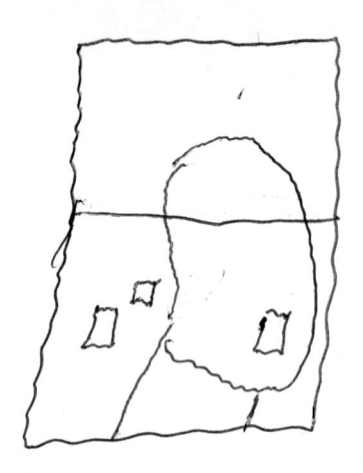